# BEHIND THE LEGEND

little bee books

An imprint of Bonnier Publishing USA
251 Park Avenue South, New York, NY 10010
Copyright © 2018 by Bonnier Publishing USA
Cover illustration by Victor Rivas

Manufactured in the United States LAK 1217

Library of Congress Cataloging-in-Publication Data
Names: Peabody, Erin, author. | Tejido, Jomike, illustrator.
Title: Unicorns / by Erin Peabody; illustrated by Jomike Tejido.
Description: New York: little bee books, 2018. | Series: Behind the legend
Includes bibliographical references. | Audience: Ages 8–10.
Identifiers: LCCN 2017038867 (print) | Subjects: LCSH: Unicorns—Juvenile literature.
BISAC: JUVENILE NONFICTION / Social Science / Folklore & Mythology. | JUVENILE
NONFICTION / Animals / Horses. | JUVENILE NONFICTION / Science & Nature /
Discoveries. | Classification: LCC GR830.U6 (ebook) | LCC GR830.U6 P43 2018 (print)
DDC 398.24/54—dc23 | LC record available at https://lccn.loc.gov/2017038867

ISBN 978-1-4998-0575-8 (hc)
First Edition 10 9 8 7 6 5 4 3 2 1
ISBN 978-1-4998-0574-1 (pbk)
First Edition 10 9 8 7 6 5 4 3 2 1

littlebeebooks.com
bonnierpublishingusa.com

## BEHIND THE LEGEND

# UNICORNS

by Erin Peabody

art by Jomike Tejido

little bee books

# CONTENTS

Introduction
**MEET THE MONSTER**.................1

Chapter One
**ONE-HORNED WONDER** ..............9

Chapter Two
**HOLY HORSE** ......................35

Chapter Three
**OF POWER AND POISON**............57

Chapter Four
**A BEAUTY SCRUTINIZED** ...........73

Chapter Five
**DOUBTERS AND DREAMERS**.........89

Conclusion
**KEEP YOUR SPARKLE** ............115

**MAIN SOURCES**....................120

**FOR FURTHER READING**............121

## INTRODUCTION

# MEET THE MONSTER

[Alice]: "Do you know, I always thought Unicorns were fabulous monsters, too! I never saw one alive before!"

"Well, now that we *have* seen each other," said the Unicorn, "if you'll believe in me, I'll believe in you."

—Lewis Carroll, *Through the Looking Glass*

W hat could possibly be more magical than unicorns? Gleaming white creatures with sparkly eyes and flowing manes—these prancing pretties leap with abandon through our imaginations. They beckon us to misty, faraway lands and rainbow-filled skies. Astride these good and trustworthy guides, we feel safe and secure. Life is fun and free.

And that horn! Spiraling like a perfect seashell, the horn sprouting from the unicorn's head radiates might and wisdom. With lengths ranging from twelve inches to a whopping seven feet (holy unicorn!), these horns astound. Even more stunning are this slender spire's alleged powers. It's been thought to cure disease, destroy enemies, and serve as an everlasting good luck charm.

In this book, we'll investigate these marvelous claims, plus many others. We'll journey to faraway lands from ancient history where travelers believed unicorns dashed and darted among rhinos and elephants. We'll explore distant castles and peer inside the curiosity cabinets (also known as wonder cabinets, or *wunderkammern*) kept by kings and queens, which featured rare and exotic specimens from nature—skulls, stuffed peacocks, dried crocodiles—and real stunners, like mermaid skins and unicorn horns! We'll learn about unicorn scholars and about scammers who made ugly money from these beautiful creatures. And we'll wade through the deadly, tainted waters of the medieval era, where no chalice or cup was safe from poison.

A solitary wonder, the unicorn stands out among the world's legendary creatures. Unlike dragons, werewolves, zombies, and a host of other scary monsters, the unicorn is one of the *only* beasts we've imagined to be noble, fair, and good.

Or *did* we imagine it? Is it possible that these larger-than-life, horned equines were real and once ran wild across deserts, mountains, and moors? Could they still?

Today's pink, fluffy unicorns are the descendants of a mysterious and wondrous beast. Using our brains, hearts, and imaginations, let's go find it!

Imagine you travel back in time to ancient Greece. A book lover—and a famous thinker in your own right—you head to the library. Walking past a series of columns, you enter the giant stone structure. You stroll through hallowed halls, past serious men in tunics and robes. Women were prohibited from entering such public spaces. (And we thought those ancient Greeks were civilized!) All around you, shelves are stacked with scrolls, some so high they require a ladder to reach.

Given this magical opportunity—to travel back in time to around 400 BCE—what book do you hunt for? For what rare (and now possibly missing!) papers do you search?

You hunt for a book . . . on unicorns, of course!

Good instincts! Believe it or not, there's a good chance that a visitor to an early library could have found information about unicorns.

However, the reading material you (or they) found wouldn't be a book in a modern sense. It would be a rolled-up scroll with handwritten words and pictures on it. This early paper material was called papyrus and was made out of a plant with the same name. Had you unrolled this paper, you would have been stunned to read descriptions of strange, hoofed creatures from faraway lands.

# A WILD WHAT?!

These horselike animals were first referred to as "wild asses." (Pardon us, unicorns!) They were beautiful, with white bodies, dark red heads, and eyes the color of the sea. The horn mounted to the beast's forehead—pure white with a bright red tip—was said to possess unique healing properties. And according to the earliest written accounts on unicorns, they were also "exceedingly swift and powerful" and defied capture. No other creature on earth could run faster.

So who was the lucky writer who first wrote about such amazing beasts? He was the Greek scholar and physician Ctesias. Around 400 BCE, Ctesias volunteered, or was forced—historians don't know for sure—to travel to Persia (today's Iran) to serve as the personal doctor to the Persian king Artaxerxes II Mnemon. (Try saying that name three times fast!) Ctesias enjoyed decent comfort, we can suppose, since he was afforded time to mingle freely and chat with Persian officials and visitors. Yet he also saw his share of drama, including one instance in which he scored big points with the king. When Artaxerxes II's power-hungry brother Cyrus attacked the king with a javelin and nearly killed him, Ctesias rushed in and successfully treated the Persian leader, thus saving the day!

During his several years in Persia, Ctesias spoke with many travelers from distant lands. They told him stories of marvelous creatures and peoples. An educated man, Ctesias felt obliged to share these curious details with others. So, upon returning home to Greece, he got busy writing the stories down. *Really* busy.

By the time Ctesias was finished, he had written twenty-three books on the history of Persia, and one book, *Indica*, on the vast country we now call India. To ancient Greeks, India was a mysterious and exotic region known for gold, spices, and brilliantly colored fabrics. And it's here in Ctesias's *Indica* that we find those first amazing descriptions of wild asses, or, as they're now more pleasantly known, unicorns.

# THE ROMANS' "MR. KNOW-IT-ALL"

In ancient times, one of the greatest observers of the living world was the naturalist Pliny the Elder (23–79 CE). Sure, the name Pliny may sound wimpy, but this Roman was a serious scholar. Like an ancient-day Siri or Alexa, Pliny knew (and wrote about) almost *everything*.

In one of his most famous works—a thirty-seven-book series called *Naturalis Historia*—Pliny covers all kinds of topics, from artwork and animals to geography and human medicines. In this whopping masterpiece, he also mentions the unicorn, or *monoceros* (Greek for "single horn"). The enchanting animal, Pliny tells us, possessed a three-foot-long horn and made deep bellowing sounds. Whoa!

# MORE UNICORNS

Over the years, more unicorn accounts shuffled in. None other than the famous Greek thinker Aristotle (384–322 BCE) also wrote about a creature that sounds suspiciously like a unicorn. The animal, a "he-goat," Aristotle wrote, was observed "skimming over the whole earth without touching the ground." And jutting from its forehead, he added, was a "prominent horn."

Perhaps the most famous man of the ancient world, Roman leader Julius Caesar (100–44 BCE) also wrote about unicorns! He describes the large beast in *Bellum Gallicum*, his book about the wars that he waged against the people of ancient France and Belgium. The book was written in Latin, but according to a translation, Caesar's unicorn looked like an ox with an exceptionally long horn pointing from its forehead. Supposedly, this astounding creature trotted and neighed across the mysterious Hercynian Forest, a region encountered by Caesar during those Gallic wars.

Fast-forward a few hundred years, and another Roman was writing extensively about unicorns. The author and early scientist was Aelian of Praeneste (170-235 CE), although, like some ancient celebrity, he went simply by his first name, Aelian. Intrigued by the natural world, Aelian wrote a series of books called *De Natura Animalium* (Latin for "On the Nature of Animals"). In one of the volumes, he refers to a group of remarkable horned creatures he calls "wild asses." Sound familiar?

As you might recall, Ctesias (who lived about five hundred years earlier than Aelian) also wrote colorfully about wild asses. Aelian's descriptions are noticeably similar. He describes the unicorn as a fierce fighter that will deploy horn, hoof, and tooth to defend itself. Its horn is striking and consists of three colors: white at the base, black in the middle, and crimson (or deep red) on top. He tells us that unicorns were hunted for these pointy gems, which were used as drinking vessels. But only "great men," Aelian says, were allowed this privilege.

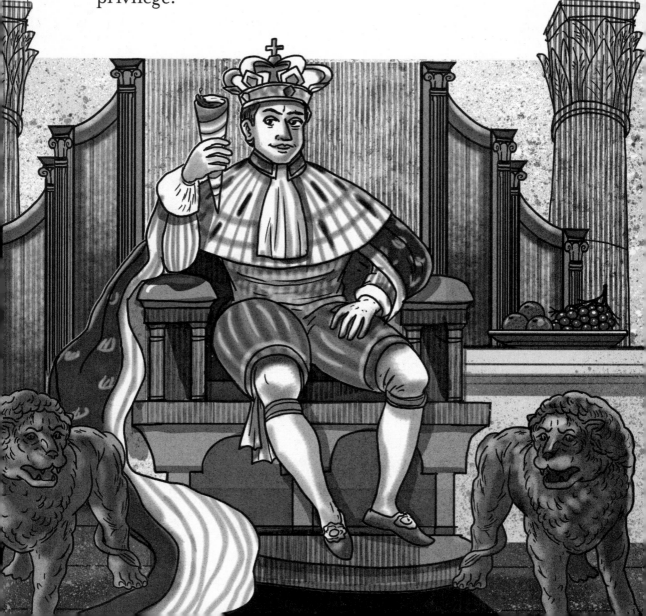

# ROLL THE BONES

Early Greeks and Romans valued animals, like unicorns, for a variety of reasons. One of the odder discoveries the ancients made was that certain bones belonging to hoofed animals were fun to play with. Wacky? Yes! But you've surely played with modern versions of these "bones" yourselves!

Somewhere along the way, a person discovered that the ankle bones of sheep and oxen were uniquely cube-shaped. And that if a person tossed one of these bones on a table or the ground, it had the interesting habit of always falling onto one of its six sides.

Any clue what these bones were used as?

Dice! The roughly cube-shaped and bone-colored dice came in a variety of sizes, depending on the size of the animal. And just like us, early people used them to play games. Fortune-tellers and vision seekers also consulted early dice to "read" the future and make tough decisions. (Kind of like how we use a Magic 8-Ball!)

# UNICORN MATH

Do you know how long a *cubit* is? In ancient times, before tape measures and rulers, people used their body parts to take measurements. So can you. Looking at your arm, trace your finger from the tip of your middle finger down the back of your arm to the tip of your elbow. That, my young Greek scholar, is a cubit. Like today's foot, yard, or meter, the cubit was a common unit for measuring length. While arm length differs from person to person, a cubit was generally considered to be eighteen inches.

The cubit was a hot topic of conversation when it came to unicorns. That's because, according to ancient texts, the animal's horn length ranged widely. The Greek physician Ctesias pegs the unicorn horn at one cubit, Aelian at one cubit and a half, and Pliny the Elder at two cubits. Other writers come in at three, four, five . . . up to *seven* cubits long! The poor unicorn that had to haul around that horn!

# A GAME OF TELEPHONE?

What do you think about these early references to unicorns? Notice any similarities among the authors' descriptions?

Today's unicorn researchers (Yes, there are people who research unicorns!) wonder if these historical accounts might share the same origins. In other words, was the unicorn story that started with Ctesias simply passed along from scholar to scholar—each man adding minor details along the way? If so, then skeptics argue, these early unicorn writings don't hold much value.

Skeptics also claim that Ctesias was a fanciful writer who was prone to exaggeration. We may have to concede some of his facts, at least a little. At one point the curious Greek doctor writes about the existence of "dog-faced" people and also men with feet so big they could use them as umbrellas! He also mentions the manticore, a creature with a man's face, three rows of teeth, and a scorpion-like tail! (*Really*, Ctesias?)

On the other hand, maybe these very old unicorn stories, repeated over and over, reveal a consistency—a pattern that lends strength to the unicorn argument. It's also important to note (in defense of Ctesias, too) that in ancient times, it was *totally* acceptable to believe in and write down the observations of other people, including strangers. Information about faraway lands was scarce. Sharing data was helpful and common.

In addition, long ago, the idea of investigating a claim or conducting independent research did not exist. And the one ancient who came closest to conducting actual science, Aristotle, seems to have left the door wide open on the possibility of unicorns. . . .

As for dog-faced people? Not so much.

## CHAPTER TWO

# HOLY HORSE

"The unicorn . . . will go up to a seated damsel
and go to sleep in her lap."
—Leonardo da Vinci, Italian artist, scientist, inventor, and author

Unicorns have a way of showing up in history's most important books—including the Bible.

That's right! In at least one of the King James versions of this holy book, the unicorn is mentioned nine times! Here's an example from the Book of Psalms, in the Old Testament: "But my horn shalt thou exalt like the horn of the unicorn" (92:10, KJV). The horn here likely represents strength, endurance, and a capacity to conquer evil.

What's interesting, too, is *how* the unicorn is referenced in the Bible. The animal doesn't conduct any miracles, nor does it fly across the heavens wearing a radiant halo. No, the Bible's unicorn is a very normal, *no-big-deal* kind of animal. It's mentioned (yawn . . .) alongside sheep, bulls, and lions.

Just like the unicorn of ancient Greece and Rome, the Bible's unicorn is also strong, swift, and fierce. And, if we believe one version of a famous Bible tale, the unicorn also had a reputation for getting a little rowdy.

# PLAYFUL PONIES

Most readers know the Bible's Old Testament story of Noah and his ark. In anticipation of a huge flood, Noah heeds God's advice and builds an enormous ark that can house two of each kind of animal. Quite impressively, Noah summons all the earth's animals and they dutifully, one by one, file into the ark.

But, according to a funny Hebrew folktale, not all the animals enter peacefully. Two holdouts, a pair of unicorns, refuse to listen to Noah. Instead, they gallop about and play unicorn games. The impertinent horsies try Noah's patience. With the rains coming and no time to spare, Noah pulls up the plank and closes the ark's door.

Tales differ on the fate of the frolicking unicorns. In one version, the unicorns swim across the rising waters until they finally die of exhaustion. In another, the unicorns are towed behind the ark from long cords which are fastened to their horns.

What do you think the moral of this humorous tale is? Were the unicorns disobedient? Or just free-spirited beasts that wished to remain wild?

# OH THEM SILLY UNICORN

Shel Silverstein—author and illustrator of such kids' favorites as *A Light in the Attic* and *The Giving Tree*—apparently also delighted in unicorns. Inspired by the silly Hebrew folktale about the rollicking, whimsical creatures, Silverstein wrote the poem "The Unicorn," found in *Where the Sidewalk Ends*.

Silverstein dreams up another unicorn in his book of poems called *Falling Up*, but this creature is not *nearly* as fun. While the unicorn finds itself in a most unfortunate predicament (its horn is stuck in a tree!), you hardly feel sorry for it. Demandingly, the animal peppers its would-be rescuers with numerous questions: Are you qualified to remove horns? How quickly can you act? Are your hands clean? By the end, even the biggest unicorn fan is left exasperated!

# A GENTLER CREATURE

Over time, however, Christians gave the unicorn of Ctesius's day a makeover. The powerful, bucking unicorn of ancient times was transformed into a pure and gentle creature. It pranced through meadows (carefully avoiding any flowers!) and cozied up to fair maidens. In images and pictures, Christians portrayed the animal as a white, sleek, and mild creature that still retained its splendid horn. Yet these changes had little to do with any physical evidence gathered—for example, sightings of white, sleek, and horned animals—and more to do with using unicorns to tell great stories.

It wasn't unusual long ago (particularly, the third century in Europe) for people to assign symbols and meaning to animals. Religious people, especially, employed animals as powerful characters in their stories. Humans, in fact, have been concocting tales about creatures since antiquity. In fact, the ancient Greek slave Aesop is famous for his animal stories that have a moral, or underlying purpose.

Some of the animals in these medieval Christian stories were bizarre-sounding. They included crocodile-like dogs, serpents with feet, and centaurs, which were men with horse bodies. Early Europeans also wrote about—and very much believed in—the dragon, the griffin (a lion with the head, wings, and front claws of an eagle), and the unicorn. The dragon was viewed as decidedly savage and wicked, while the unicorn was portrayed as pure and kind. Even today, we still unfairly assign qualities to animals: Snakes are sneaky, lions are ferocious, and doves are peaceful. Yet all are wild creatures that can't help their natural instincts, whatever they may be!

Western believers were so enthralled by these wacky creatures that they incorporated them into all kinds of art. Graceful and gentle, the unicorn soon became a very popular subject, too. That's why all across the western world today you can find images of lovely unicorns in old paintings, tapestries, and stained glass. Among the most famous unicorn-inspired works are the "Unicorn Tapestries," now located at the Metropolitan Museum of Art in New York City. These brightly colored tapestries, woven between 1495 and 1505 and made of wool, silk, and silver threads, feature the era's typically meek and mild unicorns. On one tapestry, a unicorn appears so tame and submissive that it's tethered to a pomegranate tree and enclosed by a fence.

# THE BEST BEASTLY TALES

Early Christian animal stories were full of morals and purpose, much like *Aesop's Fables*. Aesop was a slave—a brilliant one, presumably—who lived in ancient Greece sometime in the sixth century BCE. He's credited with telling many magnificent tales, some so memorable that they were passed along by word of mouth from generation to generation. Over time, people started writing them down, and eventually Aesop's stories were published, allowing us to enjoy them today.

Among Aesop's best-known stories are "The Ant and the Grasshopper," "The Fox and the Grapes," "The Dog and His Reflection," and "The Crow and the Pitcher." The tales are unique and clever and feature a moral about the consequences of, say, being foolish, greedy, or impatient. If you haven't read them already, head to your local library and grab a book featuring them!

# SACRED IN THE FAR EAST, TOO

Unicorn-like beasts also feature in ancient stories and legends from China and Japan. This creature, known as a *kirin* or *qilin*, possessed one horn, or maybe two, and was considered sacred. Even a fleeting glimpse of the stunning creature was thought to bring good fortune. According to legend, a unicorn foretold the birth of one of China's wisest and most important figures. The mother of Kong Qui allegedly spotted a unicorn before giving birth to her son, the man we now famously know as Confucius.

Probably born in 551 BCE, Confucius was an inspiring teacher and statesman. His philosophy and teachings were based on *ren*, a form of kindness and compassion. He is credited with creating a version of the Golden Rule: "What you do not wish for yourself, do not do to others."

# LOST IN TRANSLATION

Many of the world's peoples believed in some version of the unicorn well into the 1700s. Ancient religious texts, including the Bible, even reference the creature. Is this proof, do you think, that unicorns once existed?

It's hard to say. Whenever we consult old books (especially *really* old books), it's important that we interpret them with care. We cannot know with certainty what people from thousands of years ago thought or meant. As for the Bible, many, many writers contributed to the ancient book. The texts of the Old Testament, in which unicorns appear, were originally written in Hebrew, then translated into Greek, then Latin, *then* into English. Is it possible a language error occurred?

This is something to keep in mind as we continue to learn about early people and unicorns.

## CHAPTER THREE

# OF POWER AND POISON

"His horn
Bursts from his tranquil brow
Like a comet born."
—Anne Morrow Lindbergh, from the poem
"The Unicorn in Captivity"

**B**ecause the unicorn was an important religious symbol in the Middle Ages (through about the 1500s), it wasn't long before the royals of that era started to fawn over the one-horned beauties, too. Kings and queens craved the rare and wondrous, and unicorns, of course, fit that description perfectly.

Royalty's infatuation with the unicorn was centered on one thing: the animal's stunning horn. Just as it had in the Bible, the horn continued to symbolize power and strength. For this reason, royal families chose to personalize their coats of arms (a fancy symbol representing them) with unicorns. Unicorns were also linked to knights. After all, the two had much in common: Both had a reputation for being courageous, chivalrous, and of course, attracted to pretty young maidens.

# SYMBOL OF STRENGTH

Other powerful and noble animals with aristocratic ties included the lion, bull, boar, antelope, greyhound, and dragon. The most famous kings (like Richard I, also known as "the Lionheart," and Henry VIII) and queens (like Mary and Elizabeths I and II) used one or more of these animals as showy symbols on their coats of arms. Looking very regal, with crowns atop their heads, the lion and unicorn appear together on the royal coat of arms of the United Kingdom. In this fancy image, the lion symbolizes England and the unicorn Scotland.

Legend has it that the animals battled for the top spot, or crown, as this old English nursery rhyme suggests:

*The lion and the unicorn*

*Were fighting for the crown.*

*The lion beat the unicorn*

*All around the town.*

# MIRACLE HORN

Royalty demanded unicorn horns for other purposes. Toward the end of the Middle Ages, a unicorn horn wasn't only valued as symbol, it was also hailed as a miracle drug that could cure almost any illness or ailment. This meant big money for the guy who owned the apothecary, or drugstore, in town.

According to one medieval physician, a horn was an effective treatment "for all poisons, for fevers, for bites of mad dogs and scorpions, for falling sickness, worms, fluxes, loss of memory, the plague, and prolongation of youth."

Poison, you might wonder? Yes, apparently, death by poisoning was a common way to die during medieval times. In addition to the plague, famine, and mad scorpions, the poor people of sixteenth- and seventeenth-century Europe also had to worry about death by poison! It was not unusual for someone to "off" his enemy by sneaking a deadly herb into a man's chalice, or cup.

So, where did a sinister and plotting medieval person go to get their poison?

If you were a young woman living in Italy during the early seventeenth century, you just might have sought the help of the infamous poison peddler Giulia Tofana. Women had few rights at the time, so if they felt trapped in an unhappy marriage—or worse, were being abused, or hurt, by their husbands—they might have gone to Tofana to plan an escape.

Tofana tried to keep her poisonous potion, known as "Aqua Tofana," a secret. She sold it as a cosmetic. And so no one was suspicious, one of her deadly formulas came in a bottle decorated with a picture of the kind and generous St. Nicholas. Sneaky lady!

The woman blamed for causing an estimated six hundred deaths was eventually put to death herself. However, if it's true that Tofana often helped people who were victims, then the famous poison lady saved many lives, too.

Because of their enormous power (and because they could be royal tyrants!), kings and queens were common targets for poisoning. Aware that they were in danger, the well-to-do spent a pretty penny (and pound) to guard their lives. As was mentioned above, horns, especially unicorn horns, were considered the best protection against poison.

Any king or queen worth their salt kept a horn at close distance. These treasures, which cost a small fortune and were often coated in gold, were typically kept in curiosity cabinets, also known as curios, which contained a dazzling array of other weird specimens, including stuffed birds, preserved reptiles, and the bones and skulls of animals— and humans! To ensure her safety, a queen could either sip out of her personal unicorn horn, or be administered a bit of powder filed from the horn. The proper dose according to one medieval herbalist, was "four grains to half a scruple." (A scruple, by the way, is equal to about twenty grains. It was a common measurement used in ancient pharmacies.)

Medieval folks had some weird ideas about medicines. They had a good excuse, given the thousands of people at the time dying from the plague, poisons, and other causes. Imagine if several people you knew died from a mysterious and powerful killer, and no one could understand the cause of it or how to prevent it. Desperation led people to experiment with strange substances. What about you? If your doctor told you that snake flesh would guard against death, would you try it? Other so-called "drugs" at the time included: elk and deer hoofs, scorpion "dust," viper's flesh, and birds' hearts. . . . Yuck!

The unicorn horn, people thought, could save lives. It was a stunning, splendid prize to show off when other royalty came to visit. Because of its extraordinary value (worth ten times its weight in gold!), the unicorn horn was hunted fiercely in medieval times.

We'll soon find out what this meant for the magical beast with the precious horn.

CHAPTER FOUR

# A BEAUTY SCRUTINIZED

"O Unicorn among the cedars,
To whom no magic charm can lead us."
—W. H. Auden, from the poem "New Year Letter"

Animals with horns might as well have targets on their backs. Since early on (and even today), magnificent creatures with horns and tusks—including rhinos, elephants, and narwhals—have been hunted.

Sometimes the hunter kills just for the horn, to own it and proudly put it on a shelf. Other times, as we've discussed, people hunt creatures like the unicorn out of desperation. Dying from strange diseases, people in medieval times were willing to try anything, including powder from a unicorn horn.

These early victims fervently hoped that a unicorn horn would save them. How sad it must have been when it didn't.

# FAKE HORNS

Horns fetched big money. Sellers could make a fortune, so it wasn't long before cheaters arrived on the scene and starting selling fake horns that they claimed came from unicorns. Potential buyers were advised to run "tests" on horns to try and tell fake ones from the real ones. The tests were crude and not scientific. One involved dipping a horn in water and watching for it to bubble. Bubbles, early observers believed, were a sign that the material was genuine.

Since one of the major features of the unicorn horn was thought to be its ability to neutralize, or cancel out, poisons, and because this was becoming such a big business, in the early 1600s, a professor and a physician decided to see if a horn could, in fact, stop poison. Their experiment involved giving poison to two kittens, which were then treated with powdered horn. Sadly, the kittens died, but there were some positive outcomes. Starting in the 1600s, educated people began to realize that expensive horns didn't have medicinal value. As a result, more people practiced smarter medicine, and fewer animals were hunted for their horns.

But progress is slow. Traditions die hard. Even today, some cultures from around the world continue to believe in animal cures—for instance, that rhino horns can cure cancer. However, such beliefs are totally unproven and can actually harm both human health and wildlife populations.

# SUPERSTITION HURTS WILDLIFE

Most superstitions are harmless: "Step on a crack—you'll break your mother's back." Or the idea that seeing a penny and not picking it up will bring bad luck. We laugh at these silly sayings and notions because we know that they're false.

However, some ancient beliefs endure and can be harmful to wildlife. Just like demand for unicorn horns, there are some cultures around the world that continue to value the horns and tusks of rhinoceroses, elephants, and other wildlife. And many, without access to modern medicine, mistakenly believe that horns and tusks can cure ailments ranging from fever to cancer. (We're talking about people living today—in modern times!)

These false beliefs are basically rumors. They're inaccurate, dangerous, and hard to stop. And the demand for horns puts stress on fragile animal populations, especially rhinos and elephants.

It's better for us all—our health, our planet, and all wildlife— when we spread facts, not falsehoods!

# PEER PRESSURE DURING THE RENAISSANCE

It didn't go over well when early scientific types, like French doctor Ambroise Paré (1510-1590), started to publish writings that were skeptical of unicorn horns, especially their so-called value as medicine. People were shocked when Paré, for instance, wrote that unicorn horns were completely useless against all poisons.

During the early 1600s in Europe, most people lived their lives according to tradition and religion. Science was new. And while innovation during the Renaissance period brought exciting advances (like the clock and the flush toilet!), most folks didn't like serious scientists showing up and doubting their culture's long-held beliefs.

The French doctor Paré experienced this resistance when he declared that the unicorn horn was *not* magical. He ran numerous "bubble tests," dunking several different kinds of horns under water. All the horns—whether from cows, goats, or sheep—bubbled. So did ordinary objects, like the covers of pots and pieces of wood!

People balked and responded angrily upon hearing this. To which Paré replied (in French, of course): "I should prefer to be right entirely alone than to be wrong . . . with all the rest of the world."

What about you? Are you willing to stand alone with your beliefs, even if they differ from everyone else's?

In terms of unicorn horns, you would have been wise to side with Paré. Many medieval-era people risked drinking from poisoned cups because they believed a unicorn horn would save them. Sadly, these foolish souls ended up dead.

Okay, so Paré didn't believe in the medicinal powers of unicorn horns. But (spoiler alert!) he didn't exactly believe in unicorns themselves, either. And he wasn't alone.

Starting in the sixteenth century, more and more serious thinkers began to doubt that unicorns existed at all, including the French priest and explorer André Thevet (1502–1590). At a time when most people didn't venture out of their villages, Thevet was traveling the globe, learning about the people and wilds of Europe, Egypt, and Brazil. So when this worldly scholar wrote a book, *Cosmographie Univerelle*, which included a chapter devoted to unicorns, more than a few readers took notice. Especially stunning: The religious man declared the unicorn horn of queens' castles and cathedral closets a total fake—nothing more than a product of deception and lies.

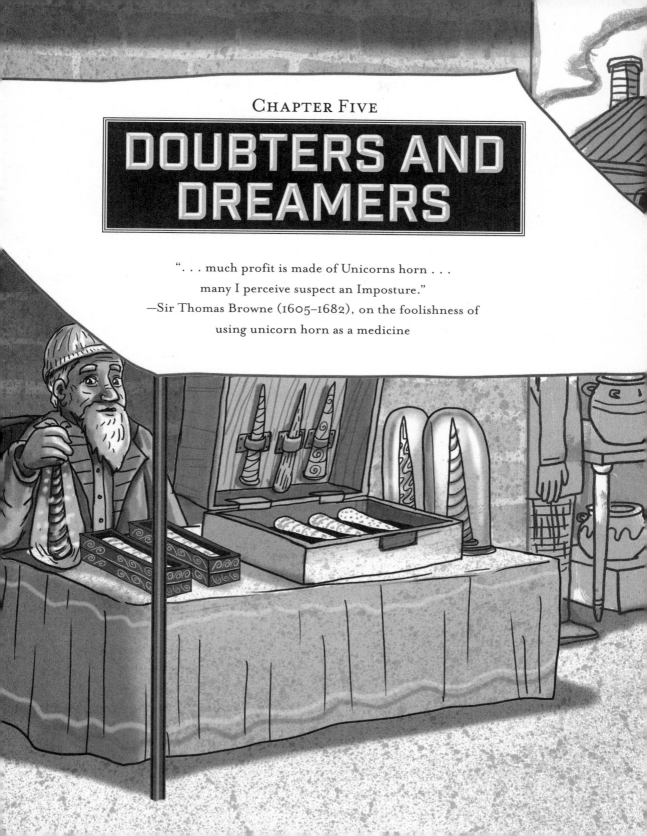

## CHAPTER FIVE

# DOUBTERS AND DREAMERS

"... much profit is made of Unicorns horn ...
many I perceive suspect an Imposture."
—Sir Thomas Browne (1605–1682), on the foolishness of
using unicorn horn as a medicine

Educated and well-traveled, Thevet probably never meant to burst anyone's "unicorn" bubble, so to speak. Just like Ctesias, he felt fortunate to accrue the knowledge afforded by travel and wished to share it. The priest was also tired of seeing his fellow Europeans be made into fools. He knew there was deceit lurking in the continent's many curiosity cabinets. Thevet had seen the fakes forged firsthand.

During one of his trips, while visiting a shipping port near the Red Sea in the Indian Ocean, the curious priest saw men handling what appeared to be curvy bones. Upon closer inspection, he realized those ivory points were actually the tusks of elephants and walruses! Having figured out a way to straighten the tusks, the men were loading them onto ships and selling them for princely sums as unicorn horns!

There was more. Thevet respectfully disagreed with his brainy elders, men like Aristotle, for their unicorn confusion. As he saw it, they lacked access to "modern" knowledge (or at least what was modern to people in the 1600s). In other words, according to Thevet, it wasn't the ancients' fault if they believed in unicorns—they simply lacked the information or evidence to know otherwise. And the colorful stories about unicorns prancing in meadows and kneeling beside fair maidens? Well, those, said Thevet, were simply the chatterings of old gossip 'round the winter fire or parables meant to teach readers lessons.

# TWO KINDS OF FAITH

Yet Thevet hardly had the final word on unicorns. Across the sixteenth and seventeenth centuries, it seems that for every insistent unicorn doubter, there was a passionate unicorn believer. Some, like the Reverend Edward Topsell (1572–1625), pointed to the holy texts of the Bible as the sole—and only needed—proof that unicorns existed. Not exactly tolerant, he referred to unicorn skeptics as "vulgar." Instead of engaging in a thoughtful conversation, it seemed easier for Topsell to dismiss naysayers as simply bad, or evil. (Curiously, while Topsell seems to have adored unicorns, he despised cats, calling them "dangerous to the soul and body." Quite devout and religious, he thought cats were the playthings of witches!)

Fortunately, other more cool-headed types would enter the unicorn conversation not long afterward. These men professed a faith—not a religious one, but one rooted in scientific thought. One was Caspar Bartholin the Elder (1585-1629), a brilliant Danish scholar and professor. (He was reading by the age of three and composing Greek and Latin speeches at thirteen!) In so many words, he challenged the unicorn doubters. He begged of them, is it fair to doubt, or not believe in something, just because we've never *seen* it? For Bartholin the Elder, the earth was still full of mystery, with vast portions still uncharted and unknown to white men. *Could unicorns exist in some far-off land?* he wondered.

# GALLOPING ON

Even if we never see one, the unicorn still inspires fun, fantasy, and a great imagination. They alight on the pages of books, from the ancient to the modern. Their sleek bodies bring wondrous beauty to the world's museums—whether the creatures are painted onto canvas, woven into a bright tapestry, or sculpted out of bronze.

Unicorns have captivated some of the world's most famous artists, including the famous *Mona Lisa* painter, Leonardo da Vinci, who liked to draw unicorns. And Raphael, an Italian Renaissance artist, painted *Young Woman with Unicorn*.

Those are just the classics. Unicorns are a hugely popular subject in modern literature and art. Have you heard of the fantasy novel *The Last Unicorn* by Peter S. Beagle? Or *The Last Battle*, the seventh and final novel in the Chronicles of Narnia by C. S. Lewis? Both feature stellar unicorn characters. Other great unicorn titles appear at the end of this book.

# MARVELOUS LAND

No other place on earth compares to Africa—whether in ancient times or today. It seems to be home to the most astounding beasts, including giraffes, hippopotamuses, elephants, and rhinos. One early writer said that in Africa, "Nature puts forth the strangest forms of life." The unicorn almost seems dull compared to the magnificently strange giraffe, with its irregular spots and tree trunk of a neck, and the elephant, with its giant, flapping ears and hose of a nose. What about you?

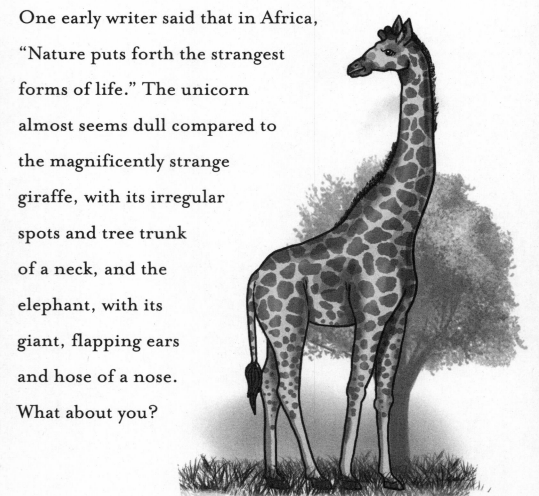

If you had never seen an elephant in a picture or a zoo and someone described one to you, would you still believe them? Even today, we're flabbergasted by nature in all its weird and wonderful forms. So it wasn't much of a leap at all, centuries ago, for people to speculate that Africa—home to lions, hippos, and rhinos—could be home to unicorns, too.

Throughout the 1700s and 1800s, explorers tromped excitedly across the continent for physical evidence of the creatures that inhabited it—including fossils, furs, and skeletons. They heard stories from local tribes about a shy, horned animal that had the qualities of both a rhino and a horse. English traveler and scientist Sir Francis Galton (1822-1911) was a unicorn skeptic before traveling to Africa in the 1840s, but upon talking to native peoples there, became nearly convinced that the mystical creature was real. He describes interviewing some local Africans at length: "I cross-questioned them thoroughly, but they persisted in describing a one-horned animal . . . whose one horn was in the middle of its forehead. . . ." He added, "It will be strange indeed if, after all, the creature has a real existence."

However, no proper unicorns have appeared, to Galton or anyone else. Africa was a land of incredible creatures, but it didn't seem to be hiding any gleaming, one-horned animals. Or was it?

# CONFUSED CREATURES

A one-horned animal that did live in Africa (and Asia) was the rhino. Its horn was viewed as magical, a miracle medicine for treating all kinds of ailments. And the powerful rhino, quick to defend itself, was hard to catch alive. Do these descriptions sound familiar?

While it may seem laughable, it's true that some unicorn researchers think that the rhino is the REAL unicorn—or more accurately, the animal that early people commonly mistook for a unicorn. But how could anyone confuse a leathery, mud-wallowing rhino with a sleek white unicorn? Well, researchers have an explanation for that, too. It's Unicorn #2: the oryx! This large antelope, once found extensively across Africa and the Arabian Peninsula, fits the unicorn description even better, with its white to buff-colored body and long, perfectly straight, pointed horns. From the side, its pair of slender horns is easy to mistake for a single one.

Far from these dry, hot lands, another creature is entangled in the unicorn legend. It's a whale, specifically the narwhal, which lives in the frigid waters around Greenland, Canada, and Russia. Its long, spiraling "horn" (which is actually a large tooth!) looks just like an imagined unicorn horn. This beautiful tooth, which ranges from about five to ten feet long, was once a favorite of hunters. Undoubtedly, many of the horns found in the curiosity cabinets of kings and queens were actually the teeth of narwhals—or "sea unicorns," as they were once called.

# "MARCO" ... "RHINO!"

It's true—cases of mistaken identity were quite common centuries ago. Imagine it: You're an explorer from long ago setting off for a strange island rumored to contain the most fantastic-sounding animals. After months of travel, you finally arrive at your destination. Excited and a little frightened, you gaze up at giant trees that block the sky. You feel the earth quake beneath your feet as herds of large beasts stampede close by. You hear strange-sounding yelps, shrieks, squawks, and coos coming from the jungle trees around you. You want to share these thrilling observations with others, but how do you describe a world that seems more imaginary than real?

At the end of the thirteenth century, famous Italian explorer Marco Polo found himself precisely in this position. While investigating today's island of Sumatra in the Indian Ocean, the brave adventurer encountered elephants and an assortment of other curious creatures. He also spied a beast with "hair like that of a buffalo, feet like those of an elephant, and a horn in the middle of the forehead, which is black and very thick."

Immediately, Polo's mind leapt to the one-horned animal about which he'd heard and read so much: the unicorn! Even after watching the animal wallow in mud, Polo was convinced he'd seen a unicorn (albeit not a very dignified one!). As time would later reveal, Polo had not seen a unicorn but a Sumatran rhino, an amazing animal no less.

You may be bummed to learn that many ancient "unicorns" were likely just rhinos, oryx, and narwhals in disguise. It's also true that modern scientists have not uncovered any bones or fossils pointing to the existence of a long-ago unicorn creature—at least not yet. However, that doesn't mean your investigations into legendary unicorns has to end. Researchers are still trying to make sense of the many ancient stories of one-horned creatures from around the globe.

And what about the narwhal, oryx, and rhino? These animals are fascinating in their own right. Did you know the narwhal uses its mega-tooth for jousting and for "reading" its surroundings? Full of nerve cells, the narwhal's twisty tooth is very sensitive, similar to our own tooth sensitivity when we—ouch!—bite into ice cream. Such a talented tooth likely helps the narwhal find food and mates and to avoid danger.

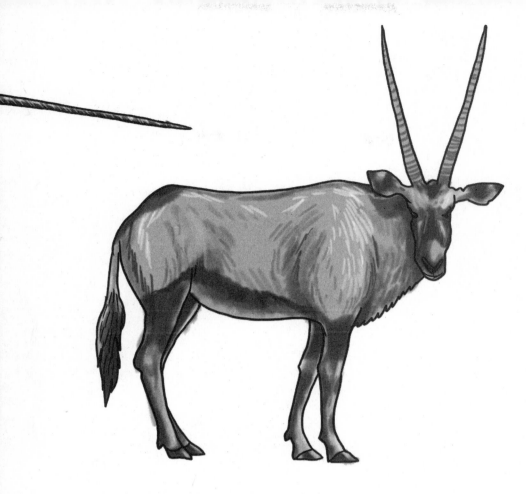

On this rich and fascinating planet, there's much more to explore. And the great thing about truth and science is that it helps animals in need. We now know that horns *cannot* rescue a person from poisoning or disease, which reduces needless hunting. And that's good news for people and for horned creatures everywhere!

# KEEP YOUR SPARKLE

"What do men know? Because they have seen no unicorns for
a while does not mean that we have all vanished."
— *The Last Unicorn* (1982) movie

Unicorns are the flowers in the garden, the icing on the cake. They're the friend who knows your best secrets—who makes you laugh when you've had a bad day. Unicorns are the little things, the almost-invisible things. Like a tiny pinch of glitter, they may be hard to see—if at all—but unicorns add definite sparkle to our lives.

While we may never see a real-life gliding unicorn, we can still be amazed by the legends surrounding this magical creature. Millions and millions of people across world history have extracted beauty, meaning, and inspiration from the unicorn. And even the doubters, in their careful, patient search for the mystical beast, have been gripped by the desire to investigate and dig up answers. Scientific inquiry can be as thrilling as dreaming.

Yet no matter how clever we are, we always need wonder in our lives. Take it from one of the most famous scientists of all time, Albert Einstein: "The most beautiful thing we can experience is the mysterious. It is the source of all true art and science." When we stop wondering, he once said, we're "as good as dead."

So do as the great scientist said: Keep dreaming. Remain curious. And don't be afraid to ask the big questions!

# MAIN SOURCES

Hague, Michael. *Michael Hague's Magical World of Unicorns*. New York: Simon & Schuster Books for Young Readers, 1999.

Johnsgard, Paul, and Karin Johnsgard. *Dragons and Unicorns: A Natural History*. New York: St. Martin's Press, 1982.

Lavers, Chris. *The Natural History of Unicorns*. New York: William Morrow, 2009.

Shepard, Odell. *The Lore of the Unicorn*. New York: Random House, 1988.

# FOR FURTHER READING

Can't get enough of the wondrous unicorn? You're not alone. Numerous authors across the decades have also been fascinated by these creatures and their magical haunts. Here is a sprinkling of titles to consider if you're in need of a unicorn "fix." As always, ask your local librarian for suggestions, too!

*The Last Battle*, the last novel in the Chronicles of Narnia by C. S. Lewis

*The Last Unicorn* by Peter S. Beagle

*A Swiftly Tilting Planet* by Madeleine L'Engle

*Into the Land of the Unicorns* by Bruce Coville

*The Unicorn Treasury: Stories, Poems, and Unicorn Lore* by Bruce Coville

*The Unicorn's Secret: Moonsilver* by Kathleen Duey

*The Little White Horse* by Elizabeth Goudge

The Unicorns of Balinor series by Mary Stanton